Welcome Message

Welcome, Mama. You're Right On Time.

We are so glad you're here.

You're holding more than an activity journal—you're holding a quiet and thoughtful parenting revolution.

By choosing to raise a child who is curious about difference, comfortable across cultures, and rooted in grace and empathy, you're making a bold and beautiful commitment. One that will ripple beyond your home and into our shared future.

This activity journal is here to help. With simple prompts, intentional questions, and everyday activities, you'll explore ways to gently expand your child's worldview—through books, conversations, media, and the moments you already share.

Some days will feel easy. Others may stretch you. Stay with it. Your consistency matters more than your perfection. This is not about getting it all right. It's about showing up, again and again, for your child—and for the world they'll help shape.

We're so glad you're here. The work you're doing is sacred, necessary, and right on time.

Let's raise a generation ready for the world—and ready to make it better.

With gratitude,

Dr. Nikki R. Lanier

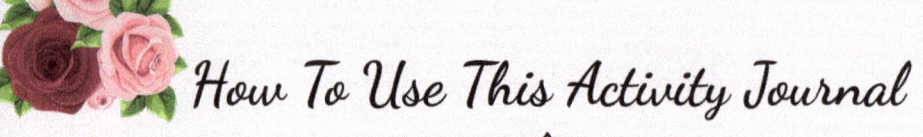

How To Use This Activity Journal

Each of the 84 activities are designed to be approachable, repeatable, and enriching. You don't need hours—you just need intention.

Each daily page includes a Prompt or Activity – A practical idea to experience with your child (book to read, song to listen to, show to watch, conversation to have, place to visit, etc.). There are lines for you to journal responses and reflections from your kiddos.

Note what you are observing happening with you as you are navigating these conversations and experiences with your children **and importantly,** what you're observing happening with them. Are they fidgety, just expressing discomfort, irritated, excited, curious? Take note of it all.

The goal is to get through all 84 of these experiences so that kids become more comfortable with these kinds of topics. The discomfort that you might notice toward the beginning is the same discomfort that many of us feel as adults because we didn't have moms like you who helped us manage these kinds of conversations before we grew up.

Keep in Mind:
◆ How you are handling this – These topics are not easy to unpack for any of us. Give yourself grace. It's OK if you don't have all the answers. What's most important is that the conversations are being had. Avoid feeling any guilt, shame, or pressure that is not yours to own. You might be surprised by what your kids already know and feel about these topics.

◆ You Have Time – There are 84 prompts to be navigated over 365 days. Don't feel compelled to do them all back to back. You may not complete them all in a year. Go easy on yourself and your kiddos. The engagement doesn't have to be continuous.

Child Engagement Moment

To keep your kiddo engaged in an activity journal experience focused on building cultural fluency, it's essential to blend play, storytelling, creativity, movement, and real-life application into the process.

Here's a suggested framework to keep their attention and make the learning joyful and meaningful:

Engagement Framework

1. SEE – Visual Stimulus: Use a book, short video, photo, or object representing a different culture or perspective.

2. SAY – Talk About It Conversationally: Use storytelling to jump start conversations and try not to be critical. You are gently shaping beliefs and norms around difference, not condemning or criticizing them for the ones they may already have unbeknownst to you.

3. DO – Hands-on Engagement: Include a creative or physical activity that connects with the theme. Things like walk and talks, role-playing, chatting while coloring, playing or even doing a puzzle are great vehicles for this.

4. FEEL – Emotional Connection: End with a short prompt that helps the child connect the experience to their own feelings or values. Emotions are usually felt seconds before we. act. Feelings matter immensely and should be acknowledged throughout these experiences.

Layered Learning for Different Ages

- Ages 4–6: Keep conversations light, use more play-based activities, include songs, puppets, and pictures. Encourage expressive art (drawing, playdough, movement).
- Ages 7–9: Introduce more structured reflection (drawing with captions, short sentences), include simple facts and comparisons.
- Ages 10–12: Encourage journaling alongside the parent, critical thinking questions, and leadership roles (teach-back activities).

Built-In Motivation Tools

- Stickers or stamp trackers – Reward participation daily or weekly.
- Progress chart– Visualize 84 activities with a colorful path or ladder to track completion.
- Mini-awards or cultural explorer badges– Celebrate small milestones with printable certificates.
- Reflection wall– Create a home display of what they've learned: photos, flags, art, words, etc.

There are few things more powerful than intentional parenting. It allows us to instill the values and characteristics in our children that we hope to see in our communities. If we want a world that prioritizes inclusiveness, it's not going to occur by happenstance. There must be a conscious effort on our part to raise kiddos that embrace difference.

You've got this. You are ready to leverage the special bond between you and your child to ensure they are ready for, and will be a meaningful contributor to, a multicultural society...

Let's Get Started!

THEME 1:

Self-Awareness & Identity
(Days 1–15)

—◈—

Helping children understand who they are and how they move through the world.

Draw a picture of your family.

What do you think is special about us?

_____

_____

_____

_____

_____

_____

_____

_____

_____

What does it mean to you to be kind?

_____

_____

_____

_____

_____

_____

_____

_____

_____

_____

Who taught you that?

_____

_____

_____

_____

_____

_____

_____

_____

Ask your child: Do you think everyone in the world lives like us?

_____

_____

_____

_____

_____

_____

_____

_____

_____

Why or why not?

_____

_____

_____

_____

_____

_____

_____

Watch a short video about kids around the world and ask: What's something you noticed that's different from your life?

_____

_____

_____

_____

_____

_____

_____

_____

Did you feel like that difference was good, bad or just different?

_____

_____

_____

_____

_____

_____

_____

Write down 3 things you're proud of about your family.

_____

_____

_____

_____

_____

_____

_____

_____

Then, discuss how other families might be proud of different things.

_____

_____

_____

_____

_____

_____

_____

_____

Have your child color in a world map. Point to places where different cultures come from and say: Let's learn about kids who live here.

_____

_____

_____

_____

_____

_____

_____

_____

_____

_____

_____

_____

_____

_____

_____

_____

_____

_____

Ask: Do you think it would be hard to be the only person who looks like you in a classroom?

_____

_____

_____

_____

_____

_____

_____

_____

Why?

_____

_____

_____

_____

_____

_____

_____

_____

Write a family mission statement that includes values like respect, curiosity, kindness, and fairness.

_____

_____

_____

_____

_____

_____

_____

_____

_____

_____

_____

_____

_____

_____

_____

_____

_____

_____

_____

_____

_____

Ask: Have you ever noticed someone being left out?

_____

_____

_____

_____

_____

_____

_____

_____

What did you do? What could you do next time?

_____

_____

_____

_____

_____

_____

_____

_____

_____

Use a mirror and ask: What do you love about yourself that has nothing to do with how you look?

_____

_____

_____

_____

_____

_____

_____

_____

_____

_____

_____

_____

_____

_____

_____

_____

_____

_____

_____

Create a "Who I Am" board with photos, words, and drawings that represent your child's story—and leave room to add others' stories too.

_____

_____

_____

_____

_____

_____

_____

_____

_____

_____

_____

_____

_____

_____

_____

_____

_____

_____

_____

_____

Talk about how your child's name came to be. Then explore naming traditions from different cultures.

_____

_____

_____

_____

_____

_____

_____

_____

_____

_____

_____

_____

_____

_____

_____

_____

_____

_____

_____

Read the book "All Are Welcome" (or a similar book) and reflect: Does our home feel like a place where all are welcome? If so, how? If not, what can we do to change that?

_____

_____

_____

_____

_____

_____

_____

_____

_____

_____

_____

_____

_____

_____

_____

_____

_____

_____

_____

Do you think all people feel welcomed and safe in their home country? Why or Why Not?

_____

_____

_____

_____

_____

_____

_____

_____

_____

_____

_____

_____

_____

_____

_____

_____

_____

_____

_____

_____

Sometimes, people have a hard time taking care of their families. Do you think it's always because they made bad choices, or could there be other reasons—like not having enough help, money, or chances to do better?

_____

_____

_____

_____

_____

_____

_____

_____

_____

_____

_____

_____

_____

_____

_____

_____

_____

_____

THEME 2:

Seeing Difference Without Fear
(Days 16–30)

———— ❖ ————

Inviting curiosity instead of
discomfort around race, culture, and
lived experience.

Ask: Have you ever met someone who looked or sounded very different from you?

_____

_____

_____

_____

_____

_____

_____

_____

What did you notice or wonder?

_____

_____

_____

_____

_____

_____

_____

_____

_____

Watch a kids' movie with diverse characters (Encanto, Turning Red, Moana) and ask: What part of their culture did you love?

_____
_____
_____
_____
_____
_____
_____
_____
_____
_____
_____
_____
_____
_____
_____
_____
_____
_____
_____
_____

Visit a grocery store in a different neighborhood and explore new foods together. Pay attention to the foods that are offered, both in quality and variety.

How do you determine who you like or don't like and who you will play with or not?

_____

_____

_____

_____

_____

_____

_____

_____

_____

_____

_____

_____

_____

_____

_____

_____

_____

_____

Listen to music from a different part of the world.
Ask: What do you feel when you hear this?

Play What if? — What if your best friend spoke a different language? What if your teacher wore a hijab?

_____

_____

_____

_____

_____

_____

_____

_____

_____

_____

_____

_____

_____

_____

_____

_____

_____

_____

Ask: What do you think racism means? Why do you think it happens? You can ask the same about sexism.

Tell your child: Sometimes people are treated unfairly because of how they look. What would you do if you saw that happen?

Watch old episodes of the Cosby Show and A Different World with your child. This helps to normalize healthy black families, and college educated young adults (counter stereotypes and narratives they will be fed otherwise).

_____

_____

_____

_____

_____

_____

_____

_____

_____

_____

_____

_____

_____

_____

_____

_____

_____

Make an age-appropriate playlist together that includes artists of various cultures. Dance it out.

Take your child to a local cultural festival or museum —virtually or in person—and ask what stood out.

Ask: If your best friend couldn't celebrate their holiday at school, how would you feel?

Watch a kids' video on MLK or Ruby Bridges.
Ask: What do you think courage means?

_____

_____

_____

_____

_____

_____

_____

_____

_____

_____

_____

_____

_____

_____

_____

_____

_____

_____

_____

_____

Try a recipe from another culture. Talk about where it's from and who might cook it.

_____

_____

_____

_____

_____

_____

_____

_____

_____

_____

_____

_____

_____

_____

_____

_____

_____

Talk to your children about the word 'equity' and share that *fair* isn't always *equal*. Let's talk about what that means.

_____

_____

_____

_____

_____

_____

_____

_____

_____

_____

_____

_____

_____

_____

_____

_____

_____

_____

_____

_____

THEME 3:

Everyday Exposure & Micro-Decisions (Days 31–49)

Building multiculturalism into family life intentionally.

Let your child choose your dining out option this week. Give him/her a list of culturally diverse restaurants to choose from and research facts about the culture/cuisine to discuss while there.

Talk about your own biases or blind spots with your child—appropriately. Share the ways that you have grown or been challenged on this topic.

_____

_____

_____

_____

_____

_____

_____

_____

_____

_____

_____

_____

_____

_____

_____

_____

_____

_____

_____

_____

Rotate dolls, action figures, and illustrated books to reflect a variety of skin tones and cultures.

Look at your child's TV shows. Ask: Do most of the characters look like you? Let's find some who don't.

_____

_____

_____

_____

_____

_____

_____

_____

_____

_____

_____

_____

_____

_____

_____

_____

_____

_____

_____

Encourage playdates with children who are racially and culturally different when possible. Let them see you engage with their parents.

Make a family reading challenge: 10 books by 10 authors of color.

_____

_____

_____

_____

_____

_____

_____

_____

_____

_____

_____

_____

_____

_____

_____

_____

_____

_____

_____

Watch a family movie about historical injustice (Hidden Figures, Selma for older kids). Talk about what has changed—and what hasn't.

_____

_____

_____

_____

_____

_____

_____

_____

_____

_____

_____

_____

_____

_____

_____

_____

_____

_____

_____

Attend age appropriate story hours, library events, or exhibits led by people of color or women.

Invite a conversation: What do you think is the hardest thing about being different in a group?

_____

_____

_____

_____

_____

_____

_____

_____

_____

_____

_____

_____

_____

_____

_____

_____

_____

_____

Show your child images of Black cowboys, Asian ballerinas, Indigenous athletes—break stereotypes.

Ask: If we could take a trip anywhere in the world to learn about new people, where would you go?

Let your child hear you gracefully addressing bias when it comes up at the dinner table, in media, or in conversation.

Ask: Are you comfortable with having a point of view that your friends don't agree with? Why or Why Not?

_____

_____

_____

_____

_____

_____

_____

_____

_____

_____

_____

_____

_____

_____

_____

_____

_____

_____

_____

_____

Invite teachers to include multicultural stories or holiday mentions in the classroom.

Watch ads or shows together. Ask: Do you see different types of people in this show?

Create a culture jar. Each week, pull a country, race, religion or culture to learn something about it.

_____

_____

_____

_____

_____

_____

_____

_____

_____

_____

_____

_____

_____

_____

_____

_____

_____

_____

_____

Look at schoolwork. Ask: What cultures or histories seem to be missing from what you're learning?

Do a mini-research project together on one of the following laws and why it was passed (Title VII of the Civil Rights Act, The Voters Rights Law of 1965, The Equal Pay Act)

_____

_____

_____

_____

_____

_____

_____

_____

_____

_____

_____

_____

_____

_____

_____

_____

_____

_____

_____

_____

_____

Role play: What would you say if your friend said something hurtful about someone else?

THEME 4:

Conversation Starters & Character Building
(Days 50–64)

———⟨◇⟩———

Strengthening emotional literacy and
moral imagination.

How do you think it feels to be treated unfairly because of how you look?

What's something brave you've done lately?

How can we include kids who are usually left out?

Why do you think some people don't have friends who are different from them?

_____

_____

_____

_____

_____

_____

_____

_____

_____

_____

_____

_____

_____

_____

_____

_____

_____

_____

When have you changed your mind about someone? Can you tell me about that?

How do you know when something is unfair?

What's one kind thing you can do today for someone you don't know?

Do you think everyone's story matters? Why or Why Not?

_____

_____

_____

_____

_____

_____

_____

_____

_____

_____

_____

_____

_____

_____

_____

_____

_____

_____

_____

_____

What do you think 'feeling invisible' means? Can people be made to feel invisible?

If someone said something mean about someone else's skin or culture, what could you say and why?

_____

_____

_____

_____

_____

_____

_____

_____

_____

_____

_____

_____

_____

_____

_____

_____

_____

_____

Do you know what a stereotype is? Have you seen them occur in school or other places you go?

What do you think our family can learn from people who are different from us?

_____

_____

_____

_____

_____

_____

_____

_____

_____

_____

_____

_____

_____

_____

_____

_____

_____

_____

_____

What's one way you can be a helper in your school or neighborhood? Can you do that this week?

How would you feel if you were the only one who didn't get picked for a team or an activity? If that has happened to you, did you wonder why you weren't picked?

_____

_____

_____

_____

_____

_____

_____

_____

_____

_____

_____

_____

_____

_____

_____

_____

_____

_____

What can we do when we hear unfair jokes or comments that are hurtful to kids who are different from us?

THEME 5:

Reflection, Ritual, and Recommitment (Days 65–84)

Solidifying the habits of equity, openness, and empathy.

Make a monthly family ritual of exploring a new culture through food, film, or music.

Start a difference diary where your child writes or draws something new they learned about another culture each week. Have them note if that experience was different from, or consistent with, what they previously thought about that culture.

_____

_____

_____

_____

_____

_____

_____

_____

_____

_____

_____

_____

_____

_____

Create a culture corner at home with books, photos, and flags from around the world.

Let your child teach you one thing they've learned this week about people who are different from them.

_____

_____

_____

_____

_____

_____

_____

_____

_____

_____

_____

_____

_____

_____

_____

_____

_____

End the day with: What's one kind or fair thing you saw or did today?

Monthly check-in: What's something you now understand better than you did a month ago?

Visit places of worship that are different from your own. Without judging the experience, use this as an opportunity to discuss the role of faith by race and culture.

Ask your child to write or draw their idea of a fair world.

_____

_____

_____

_____

_____

_____

_____

_____

_____

_____

Affirm your child's journey: I'm proud of how your heart is growing. Note your emotion about their progress.

Re-watch a movie or re-read a book from earlier in the journey. What do you or your child see now that you/they didn't before?

Host a multicultural movie night with another family and discuss the differences in lived experiences you see in the film.

Ask: If someone had to describe you in 5 words, what would they say? How does that differ from how you see yourself?

_____

_____

_____

_____

_____

_____

_____

_____

_____

_____

_____

_____

_____

_____

_____

_____

_____

_____

_____

_____

Take a walk and talk about all the visible and invisible ways people are different.

Look at your child's bookshelf. What voices are missing? Make a plan to add them.

_____

_____

_____

_____

_____

_____

_____

_____

_____

_____

_____

_____

_____

_____

_____

_____

_____

End each week with: What's one thing that stretched your heart this week?

_____

_____

_____

_____

_____

_____

_____

_____

_____

_____

_____

_____

_____

_____

_____

_____

_____

_____

_____

Talk about fairness at bedtime: Where did you see someone being fair today?

Let your child write a letter to a child in another country. Try Global Penfriends.

Check out the video "Systemic Racism Explained" on YouTube. Watch it first alone and note your reaction. Then watch it with your child and note theirs.

Share one thing you wish you had learned, as a child, about race and fairness.

Make a family commitment poster about intentional inclusion: "In this house, we…"

ADDITIONAL NOTES and REFLECTIONS

ADDITIONAL NOTES and REFLECTIONS

ADDITIONAL NOTES and REFLECTIONS

ADDITIONAL NOTES and REFLECTIONS

ADDITIONAL NOTES and REFLECTIONS

www.ingramcontent.com/pod-product-compliance
Lightning Source LLC
Chambersburg PA
CBHW051639120626
46551CB00014B/2147